TEXAS

GALLERY BOOKS
An Imprint of W. H. Smith Publishers Inc.
112 Madison Avenue
New York City 10016

This edition first published in U.S.
in 1990 by Gallery Books,
an imprint of W.H. Smith Publishers, Inc.
112 Madison Avenue, New York, New York 10016

ISBN 0-8317-8839-9

Printed and bound in Spain

For rights information about the photographs in
this book please contact:

The Image Bank
111 Fifth Avenue, New York, NY 10003

Producer: Solomon M. Skolnick
Author: Jennifer Grambs
Design Concept: Lesley Ehlers
Designer: Ann-Louise Lipman
Editor: Sara Colacurto
Production: Valerie Zars
Photo Researcher: Edward Douglas
Assistant Photo Researcher: Robert V. Hale
Editorial Assistant: Carol Raguso

Title page: *The San Jacinto Monument,
east of Houston, is a 570-foot towering
reminder of the 1836 battle between
Mexico and Texas for that state's independence.* Opposite: *As this illustration
suggests, Houston is eccentric, funky,
modern, and western—a truly
cosmopolitan city.*

Think of space, lots of it—
enormous space, airy and
open, 80 percent of which
is farms and ranchland. Enrich
the space with prairies, plains,
desert, forest, lowlands, and high
mountain ranges. Imagine the
earth beneath, liquid with oil,
gushing upwards into a gigantic
western sky that sweeps over
this enormous expanse. There,
you have Texas!

This bigness is as natural to
a Texan as it is awesome to an
out-of-stater. It's not that bigger
is better to Texans; it's that
bigger is best. Most every Texan
feels that way and shares not
only this common pride, but a
fiercely independent spirit that's
as strong today as it was during
Texas' fight for independence
from Mexico in the 1830's.

The "Lone Star State"
extends more than 800 miles in
both length and breadth, adding
up to at least 2,675,338 square
miles of land. Its area roughly
equals the combined areas of
New England, New York,
Pennsylvania, Ohio, and Illinois.
Its boundaries comprise more
than seven percent of the total
land area of the U.S., and the
only state that exceeds it in size
is Alaska. With nearly 17 million
people, it's the third most popu-
lated state, surpassed only by

*The uneven skyline of Houston reflects
the diversity and sheer size of Texas'
largest city.* Following pages, left:
*Although nearly every inch of Houston
has been built upon, the city is kept
remarkably clean.* Right: *Some of
Houston's oldest, most gracious buildings still stand among the modern,
imposing structures of downtown.*

The restored homes of Sam Houston Park seem dwarfed by their tall neighbors, but in spite of that, they retain their nineteenth-century charm. Below: The Republic Bank Tower (left) is an example of the many interesting architectural styles in Houston.

Houston's Tranquility Park salutes the Apollo flights, particularly Apollo XI, the flight that included man's first moon landing. Below: A fountain of five golden, glittering rockets provides a daily shower in Tranquility Park.

California and New York, and the population seems to be growing faster than just about any other. The best way to get a grasp of Texas' size is to see it from behind the driver's wheel, and there are more than 70,000 miles of highway on which to do that.

The state motto is friendship; in fact, *thecas*—from which Texas gets its name—is a Native American word for friend. And though differences in temperament and attitude truly seem to be determined by locale, an overall powerful friendliness always prevails. "Howdy" is the greeting of choice, and a sincere interest in others' welfare is shared across the board, not just by the rugged western cowboy or cowgirl, but by East Texans and slick oil industrialists as well.

North, south, east, or west, the people and terrain of Texas are as diverse as modern movie-goers have come to believe. The prevalent cultures here are Spanish, Mexican, Native American, southern, black, suburban, and "redneck." But the differences between Texans have always had more to do with which part of Texas they call home. For the early pioneers, this was simply a matter of distinguishing between east and west, although it really is a bit more complicated than that.

The land itself really can be looked at in terms of east and west. As a matter of fact, the single most important geologic feature of Texas is the Balcones Escarpment which forms a kind of natural east-west divide. The fault extends roughly along Interstate 35—through San Antonio, Austin, and Dallas—from Mexico to Oklahoma. Warm air from the Gulf of Mexico hits the escarpment and produces rain across the southeastern part of the state. The western part of Texas gets very little rain due to this quirk of topography.

Preceding page: *The Republic Bank Tower sits in stark contrast to the adjacent twin towers of Penzoil Place. This page, top to bottom: One of Houston's many cultural attractions, the Gus W. Wortham Theater Center accommodates more than 3,000 ticket holders who come to enjoy the Houston Grand Opera and the Houston Ballet. Flags fly above the magnificent George R. Brown Convention Center. Jones Hall for the Performing Arts is the home of the Houston Symphony and the Houston Pops Orchestra.*

Many of Houston's newer buildings are geometric configurations of glass and steel. Below: *The Mellie Esperson Building is reflected on the exterior of the Texas Crude Building. Opposite: Designed by Philip Johnson and John Burgee, the Transco Tower (right) is impressive from every vantage point.*

Preceding page: *The "Texas tombstone" is better known as I.M. Pei's Texas Commerce Tower. Built in 1982, the brilliant composite tube shoots 75-stories above the skyline.* This page, above: *In 1986, Texas celebrated 150 years of statehood in Houston's Sesquicentennial Park.* Below: *A walk through Sesquicentennial Park offers a view of Houston's many architectural designs.*

But, of course, Texas is more than just a state with distinct physical characteristics. That's what makes it such a mind boggler. The regions and the distinct personalities of their inhabitants seem to form a Texas that could be divided if it ever chose to be. Ironically, an 1845 treaty allowed for the state to be divided into five states. That has never come close to happening, but nonetheless, it's intriguing to consider that, not only do natural boundaries make separation a distinct possibility, but startlingly diverse Texas attitudes characterize these regions. The common thread that binds, of course, is a massive dose of unabashed pride in being, first and foremost, a Texan.

This page, clockwise: *Artists are inspired by the many imaginative creations in Houston's parks and plazas, such as the* Virtuoso *by Adickes. The offbeat* Telephone, *also by Adickes, is another of many interesting sculptures sprinkled throughout Houston. Cowboys and skyscrapers seem to contradict one another during a rodeo parade in Houston.*

This independent spirit can be traced way back to the very beginning of Texas' history. Like many other states Texas started its life as a colony; but unlike any other state, it was its own nation before it joined the Union.

Texas had its own president and ambassadors for almost a decade before becoming the U.S.' 28th state. The red, white, and blue flag with the single star is only one of six that have flown over this vast land since Europeans first discovered it.

Texas was home to a few, mostly nomadic tribes when a Spaniard mapped its coast in 1519. But the first exploration didn't come for another nine years, when a band of Spanish sailors was marooned near Galveston and one of the survivors wrote a report about his adventures, the first written account of the area. The quest for gold spurred other Spanish expeditions—the most famous of them led by Francisco Vasquez de Coronado, who took his conquistadores as far as the Grand Canyon. More than a century went by before Spain made any attempt at colonization, starting in 1682 with a settlement at Ysleta, near El Paso. France's establishment of a short-lived outpost at the head of Lavaca Bay a few years later spurred more determined efforts

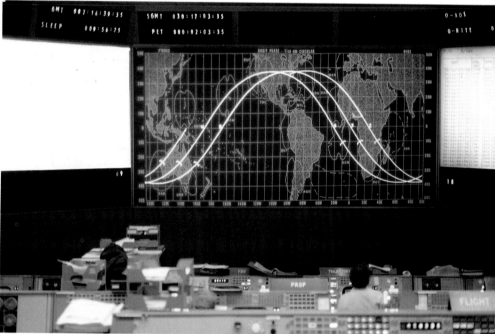

This page, top to bottom: *The Lyndon B. Johnson Space Center, south of Houston, is headquarters for America's space program. Space buffs can tour the Mission Control Center, walk through skylab and shuttle trainers, and even touch a piece of the moon at the Space Center. At the Astrodome in Houston, a stormy sky is no threat—up to 76,000 enthusiastic fans can squeeze into this enormous indoor stadium.*

by Spain, and they began sending missionaries to Christianize the natives, first in eastern Texas and later in the south-central region. These missions became seeds for the first towns, with San Antonio, Nacogdoches, and Goliad being developed by the start of the nineteenth century, when the U.S. purchase of Louisiana from France aroused American interest in the land to the west.

Spanish dominion ended in 1821, when Mexico—including Texas—broke loose from its trans-Atlantic master. Generous land grants by the Mexican government opened up Texas to a flood of settlers, especially from the southern U.S., and fifteen years after the Mexican flag was raised, there were 50,000 people living in the Texas territory, a seven-fold increase.

The dramatic increase in population began to worry Mexico, because the new American populace soon outnumbered Mexicans in Texas four-to-one. Mexico's heavy-handed attempt to cut off further American settlement and trade with the U.S. sparked a revolt in October of 1835.

The most famous battle was at a walled mission in San Antonio—and it was a defeat for the Texans. 187 Texans, including Davey Crockett, were trapped inside the Alamo by 5,000 Mexican troops. The nearly two week siege ended on March 6, 1836, when the Mexicans attacked and, within a few hours, completely wiped out the defenders.

Houston's 50-mile ship channel has made this city the third busiest ocean port in the U.S.

The defeat was avenged a month later, when the Texans routed the enemy and captured President Antonio Santa Anna at the Battle of San Jacinto. The new Republic of Texas won prompt recognition from the U.S. and European powers, which discouraged Mexico from making any determined effort to retake the land.

The Texans' first wish was to join the U.S., but the slavery issue kept them out of the Union for nine more years. It wasn't until December 29, 1845, that Texas achieved statehood. This was promptly followed by another war with Mexico, which ended three years later with the establishment of the Rio Grande as the border.

The new state's southern orientation placed it on the Confederate side in the U.S. Civil War, but Texas saw little fighting. It does, however, have the distinction of being the scene of that war's last, "unofficial" land battle. Confederates captured 800 Union soldiers at Palmito Ranch near Brownsville, deep in the Rio Grande Valley. It was the startled prisoners who informed the Confederate rebels that Lee had surrendered—a month earlier.

This page, top to bottom: *Sacred Heart Church on Galveston Island is one of a few strong buildings that survived a devastating hurricane in 1900. Much of Galveston's Victorian keepsakes are in the restored Ashton Villa. Fishing boats and cruise boats line the piers of Galveston.* Opposite: *The Bishop's Palace on Galveston's Broadway sheltered storm victims after the "big storm." Today, it is a showcase treasure owned by the Catholic diocese.*

The Nueces County Courthouse in Corpus Christi is an interesting example of the architecture in this subtropical city. Below: Less imposing is the Lichtenstein House, built in 1905.

The years following the Civil War brought a quick growth in ranching and the development of railroads in Texas. As the twentieth century began, three million people were living in the Lone Star State and agriculture dominated its economy. But cotton, wheat, and cattle were soon displaced by a gold rush of a sort the Spaniards never dreamed of—black gold.

The oil boom began with the Spindletop gusher in Beaumont in 1901. It carried Texas through the Depression and into a modern and urban age. The 1920's and 1930's brought variety, with an influx of other industries joining the oil companies in making Texas an industrial base. The years since World War II have seen further diversification, but except for occasional slumps, petroleum remains a Texas mainstay.

Corpus Christi was discovered by a Spanish explorer who named it after the religious feast day of Corpus Christi (Body of Christ). It deserves its distinction as "The Sparkling City by the Sea"; it looks out over beautiful Corpus Christi Bay and is perhaps one of the cleanest cities in the U.S. Below: Certainly one of the prettiest ports, Corpus Christi is also the deepest on the Texas coast.

The Mobil Building glows in the Dallas evening sky. **Opposite:** *Once a prairie town, Dallas has come to epitomize Texas. As the nation's eighth largest city, it is a commercial and financial center. Imposing skyscrapers bear testimony to the wealth and prestige that accompanied the city's east Texas oil strike in 1930.*

Preceding pages, left: *Like Houston, Dallas has an impressive skyline with buildings of all shapes and sizes.* Right: *Downtown Dallas.*
This page, clockwise: *The old and the new peacefully coexist in Dallas, as ultra-modern skyscrapers soar above their two-story neighbors.*
The John Neely Bryan cabin dates back to 1841, when it served as home for the city's founder and first resident. Three tall spires sit in the
forecourt of Dallas City Hall, which was designed by I.M. Pei.

There's just no simple way to describe the state's diverse geography. Not only does each area have its own distinct and remarkable features, but many of the regions overlap, blending and contrasting in very unusual ways. In general, Texas can be divided like this: the Rocky Mountains, the Great Plains, the Central Lowlands, and the Gulf Coastal Plains into which the Rio Grande Valley, Trans- Pecos, and Big Bend areas are incorporated. A visit to the far west and the Rockies will reveal the Trans-Pecos Region, steeped in old Mexican and newer American tradition because it forms the border. Here the Pecos River and the Rio Grande provide some relief from the dry, sandy expanse of the Chihuahuan Desert, with its usual amount of desert vegetation. But, surprisingly, the land eventually turns green in the higher elevations of this region, where forests of tiny Harvard Oak flourish and cantaloupe fields are tilled along the Pecos.

Preceding page: *Resembling London's Crystal Palace, The Dallas Infomart is part of the Dallas Market Center and is used by most of the country's top computer companies.* This page, above: *Historic courthouse.* Left: *Southern Methodist University is beautifully situated in the residential Highland Park area north of Dallas.*

This page, clockwise: *Dallas is headquarters for numerous multi-million dollar companies, and serves as the largest cotton trading center in the nation and the largest merchandise marketplace in the world. Constructed of iron and glass, the Infomart evokes a futuristic feeling. Music plays an important role in Dallas' cultural life.*

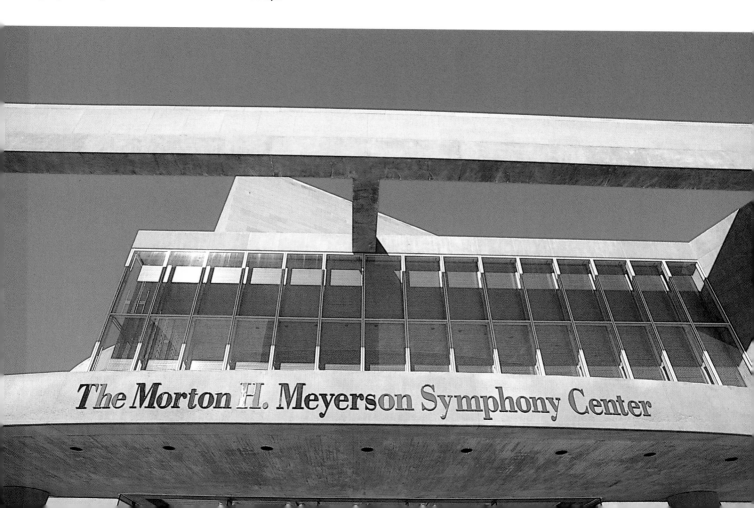

The Morton H. Meyerson Symphony Center

The State Fair of Texas is held each autumn and Texans celebrate it with their usual bravado. Below: A golden Indian points his bow skyward on the Texas State Fair Grounds.

The Guadalupe Mountains and Big Bend are Texas' two national parks and, along with the famous Rio Grande, they signal the state's proximity to Mexico. The land formations are impressive here—the 8,078-foot mass of El Capitan seems to have sprung from the earth, while farther north and deep within the earth's crust lies the prehistoric sea of oil called the Permian Basin, which is the source of much of Texas' petroleum. The forest and meadows of the area are home to elks, black bears, bighorn sheep, and mountain lions.

The Great Plains roughly begin on the western side of the Balcones Escarpment, spreading out over much of the southcentral portion of the state and up into the famous Panhandle. This part of Texas, with high plains and wheat and cotton fields in the north, can be markedly flat on the Llano Estacado or Staked Plain, but it eventually slopes gently southward to the pretty valley and hill country of the Edwards Plateau.

Texas' Central Lowlands is a rolling, 200-mile fertile area that paves the way on the south and east for the state's Gulf Coastal Plains. The plains originate as grassy marshland, often more precisely called the Coastal Prairie, in the southeast corner of the state. Inland, the plains are loaded with the hills and pine forests of east Texas and the

This page, top to bottom: *Fort Worth, sister city to Dallas, is part of the Texas Metroplex, although it has a much more wild and western flavor. The Fort Worth Stockyards area is as Cowtown as the city's nickname suggests. The Will Rogers Memorial carries on this humorist's showbiz legacy.*

The Fort Worth skyline seems to be continually changing, reflecting the industrial aspect of the city. Below: Intricately designed, the Fort Worth Water Garden draws thousands of visitors each year. Opposite: The cornerstone for Austin's State Capitol Building was laid on March 2, 1895 on the 59th anniversary of the signing of the Texas Declaration of Independence.

Located on the campus of the University of Texas in Austin, the Lyndon Baines Johnson Library and Museum is the home of more than 30 million papers from the Johnson presidency. Below: Besides historical documents, the library and museum contain exhibits which offer a glimpse of LBJ's public and private life.

Rio Grande Valley. At the Gulf of Mexico, the land melts into a 367-mile coastline, which actually swells to twice that amount of tidewater coast if bays, lagoons, and swampland are taken into account. Galveston, an island just off the coast, is remembered for the 1900 hurricane that killed about 6,000 people.

Texas is a land of many rivers, with names that are familiar to us all from western movies that we've seen: the Rio Grande, the Red, the Colorado, and the Sabine, to name some of the largest. Most of the lakes, ranging in size from tiny to enormous, like 182,000-acre Toledo Bend Reservoir (part of which is in Louisiana), are in the eastern portion of the state. At least 3,700 streams provide Texas with water, a treasured and scarce commodity.

Magnificent terrain and a unique history certainly enhance the special aura that surrounds Texas. Yet, there's more—Texan cities, parks, and attractions all have a slightly larger-than-life quality.

A recreation of the White House Oval Office, as it looked during the Johnson presidency, and Johnson's 1969 Lincoln limousine are two of the exhibits at the Lyndon Baines Johnson Library and Museum. Right: Most of Texas' governors have lived in the Greek Revival Governor's Mansion, built in Austin in 1856.

The University of Texas Tower and its adjacent fountain light up the Austin night. Below: The 17-bell carillon atop the 27-story tower is silhouetted by the setting sun. Opposite: The Spanish influence is pervasive in San Antonio, where eighteenth-century missions can be seen along the Mission Trail.

A monument in San Antonio commemorates the Alamo, where the most famous battle in Texas' fight for independence from Mexico took place. Opposite: The Alamo is part of what was originally called the Mission San Antonio de Valero— San Antonio's oldest, established in 1718. In this limestone fortress, a small but determined band of freedom fighters fought against Santa Anna's outnumbering army for Texas' independence.

This page, clockwise: *Mission San Francisco de la Espada, in San Antonio Missions National Historical Park, is protected by three-foot-thick walls. The Mission San Jose. Glistening in the sun, the eighteenth-century Governor's Palace on Military Plaza has been carefully restored. Opposite: The Rosa Window, a famous stone carving on the south side of San Jose Mission, is an outstanding feature of this 1720 structure.*

Preceding page: *A diversity of ethnic groups make up present-day Texas. All are represented at the Institute of Texan Cultures exhibits at Hemisfair Plaza—site of the 1968 World's Fair. This page, clockwise: Geronimo was once held prisoner at Fort Sam Houston, which now houses Brooke Army Medical Center, one of the largest medical facilities in the world. The spectacular River Walk, or Paseo del Rio, in San Antonio, is a charming and picturesque strip of the San Antonio River. The King William Street Historic District in San Antonio has a distinctly Victorian feel to it.*

Houston, for example, is Texas' biggest city and the fourth largest in America. Situated 50 miles inland from the Gulf, its ship channel has catapulted the city to the status of America's third busiest ship port. Named for General Sam Houston who led the San Jacinto victory, Houston is a place that has made good use of big ideas, like the 76,000-seat Astrodome, the first domed stadium ever built. Nearby are pine forests, salt marshes, swampland, and bayous, although the city itself is a flat surface with jutting superstar skyscrapers, most of them built in the last 30 years and fascinating to ponder.

The Lyndon B. Johnson Space Center, on the city's outskirts, is headquarters for America's space program. And, just to emphasize the Texas taste for importance, remember that the first word uttered on the moon was "Houston..."

This page, top to bottom: *More than a million people — mostly of Native American, Hispanic, and European descent — call the Texas border city of El Paso their home. The Tigua Indians were the first inhabitants of El Paso and many still make their home at Ysleta Mission, which adjoins their reservation. Eagles on Amistad Dam mark the U.S./ Mexican border west of Del Rio. Opposite: The Tiguas, distant cousins of the New Mexican Pueblo Indians, came to the Ysleta del Sur Pueblo sometime during the 1680's. Now living at the Ysleta reservation, this largely agricultural community is perhaps the oldest in the country.*

The Presidio La Bahia in Goliad dates back to 1749 and is the site where Mexican forces massacred Colonel James Fannin's small army. Opposite: The Texas prairie can be as colorful as it is spacious and awe-inspiring, especially when bluebonnets and coreopsis powder the surface.

Farther east, Dallas surely puts on one of the greatest shows on earth each October when it celebrates its State Fair — naturally, it's America's biggest. The former prairie town is chock full of industry (banking, insurance, and cotton production), but it was a 1930 oil strike that set the city in motion. While much of Dallas' celebrity status is a direct result of its namesake television series, a sadder notoriety comes out of the November 2, 1963 assassination of President John F. Kennedy there.

Nearby Fort Worth still retains a rugged, frontier flavor even though it is generally regarded as sister city to modern Dallas and is part of what is generally called the Metroplex. Nicknamed "Cowtown," the city, in contrast to its kin, has an old west ambience, no doubt enhanced by the restoration of the Fort Worth Stockyards.

To the south of Dallas and roughly in the center of the state, Austin is situated alongside the Colorado River in the vicinity of the Balcones Escarpment. Austin started its life as the small town of Waterloo, when it was decreed the state capital. Later, it was

Preceding page: *The Piro Indians originally built La Purisima Socorro Mission in Mexico during the 1680's, but a changing river course shifted the site to Texas, where these descendants of the great Pueblo Nation still proudly make their home. This page, top to bottom: Not all of El Paso is as new and industrious as the city's skyline might suggest. The rippling sands of the El Paso Dunes give this area a desert flavor. Stocked with wildlife and soaring to 7,192 feet at North Franklin Peak, the Franklin Mountains sometimes take on a haunting appearance.*

renamed Austin in honor of Stephen F. Austin, organizer of the state's first American settlement. The Capitol Building was finished in 1888 and, true to form, Texans still take pride in the fact that it is actually slightly taller than the Capitol Building in Washington D.C.

Perhaps the real tradition of the venerated West is most obvious in Texas' awe-inspiring scenery. Well across the state on the western edge is Big Bend National Park, with more than 775,000 acres of spectacular Texas scenery. The park embraces the soaring Chisos mountains, a massive desert expanse and, of course, the Rio Grande, with its U-shaped curve from which Big Bend gets its name.

Texas' canyons—Boquillas, Santa Elena, and Mariscal, to name the largest—are eons-old remnants of volcanic lava that formed the depths of today's canyons. In 1975, the fossil remains of a pterosaur—38-feet-wide from wing to wing—were discovered in this wild environment that, it seems, is still in the process of "being discovered."

The possibilities for experiencing Texas are enormous. A visit to the Panhandle and the Palo Duro Canyon State Park unfolds 200-million-year-old formations and an ongoing

This page, top to bottom: *Big Bend has more than 700,000 acres of high mountains, plunging canyons, and desert plains. Gentle Boquillas Canyon is mirrored by the Rio Grande. A mountain panorama as seen from Big Bend.* Opposite: *Surely the most untamed part of all the Texas wilderness is Big Bend National Park, where the jagged rock formations and deep canyons can be intimidating as well as marvelous. 17-mile-long Santa Elena Canyon on the Rio Grande inspires both emotions.*

Two thousand species of flora and fauna coexist in Big Bend, some sharing the rugged environment of Boquillas Canyon. Opposite: "The Window" of the Chisos Mountains offers a birds-eye view of earth and sky.

search for further proof of pre-Pueblo existence. West at the New Mexico-Texas border in Guadalupe Mountains National Park is Guadalupe Peak—at 8,751 feet the state's highest. Many are content to simply sit out the summer sun in one of hundreds of tiny parks that dot the miles and miles of Texas highways.

Last, but certainly not least, in the heart of Texas, sits the cosmopolitan city of San Antonio. Like no other part of the state, San Antonio manages to display a charming assortment of unique elements which have combined to form an image of the land for the rest of the country. In San Antonio, Spanish, Mexican, and American heritages blend very easily, unlike in the early days.

This is the birthplace of the independence of which Texans are so proud. Mission bells still ring out in the beautifully-preserved missions, no longer needed for defense or shelter, but simply there so Texans won't forget a time when the independent spirit that comes so naturally today was still being nourished. Davey Crockett and Jim Bowie died here. Liberty was born. And that is why Texans always proudly remember the Alamo.

Preceding pages, left: *Lost Mine Mountain in the Chisos Mountains of Big Bend National Park*. Right: *Big Bend gets its name from the U-shaped bend of the Rio Grande that dominates the Park. The river, desert, and mountain landscapes offer a diverse experience to nature lovers. These pages: The Guadalupe Mountains tower above the west Texas desert of Guadalupe Mountains National Park. El Capitan commands attention as it soars to more than 8,000 feet.*

The Red Ridge of the Quartermaster Formation, an impressive part of Palo Duro Canyon State Park, dates back to the Permian Age. Below: The Palo Duro Canyon, with its plentiful water, grass, and shelter, lured its first rancher in the 1870's. Charles Goodnight built a dugout much like this reproduction. Opposite: 200 million years of the earth's natural history is unfolded in the formations of Palo Duro, named after the juniper trees found in the area. Devil's Tombstone is a haunting part of the Trujillo Formation.

Index of Photography

All photographs courtesy of The Image Bank,
except where indicated (*).

Preceding pages: *The "Lighthouse" in Palo Duro Canyon State Park must have been astonishing to the explorer Francisco Vasquez de Coronado, who is believed to have come upon the canyon while searching for Quivira, a mythical city of gold.*